Mitsumasa Anno

ANNO'S MATH GAMES

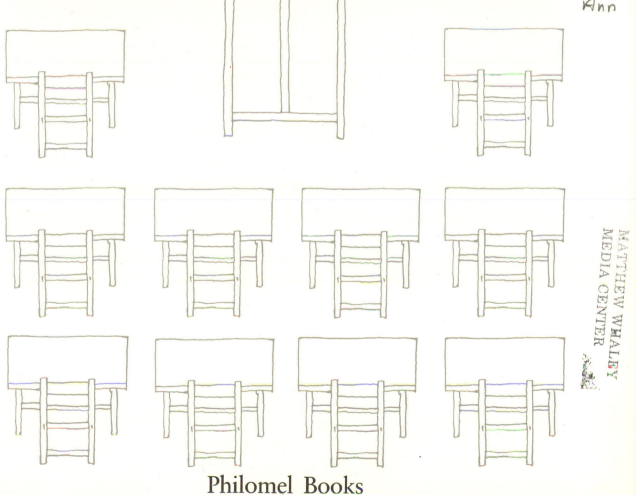

Philomel Books

Library of Congress Cataloging-in-Publication Data is at the back of this book.

▪1▪

What is Different?

There are lots of blue squares.
But there's only one red circle.
The red circle is different.
Let's look at other pictures for
things that are different.

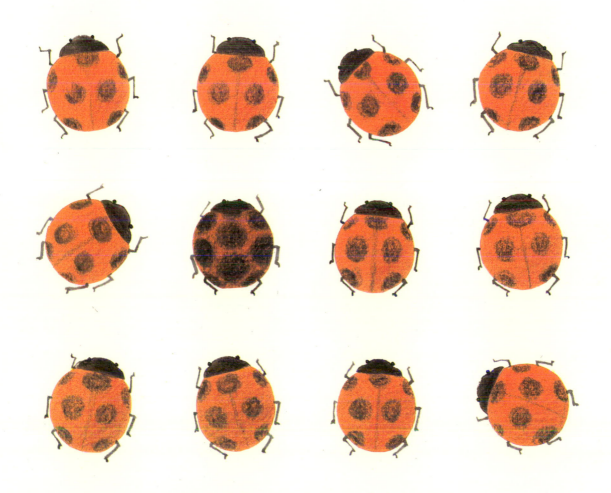

Here are lots of ladybugs.
Look carefully. One of them is different.
That ladybug stands out.
It is not like the others.

Here are lots of ducks.

Is that lonely duck at the bottom different from the rest?

No, he isn't. It's the fox at the top.

He is the one that is different.

In this picture, it's the poppy flower that is different.
It stands out because the other things in the picture
all have wings or legs and can move by themselves.
The poppy flower cannot move by itself.

Are you ready now to find the things that are different?
You can talk it over with your friends. And after you've
found which one is different, think about what it is
that makes it different.

14

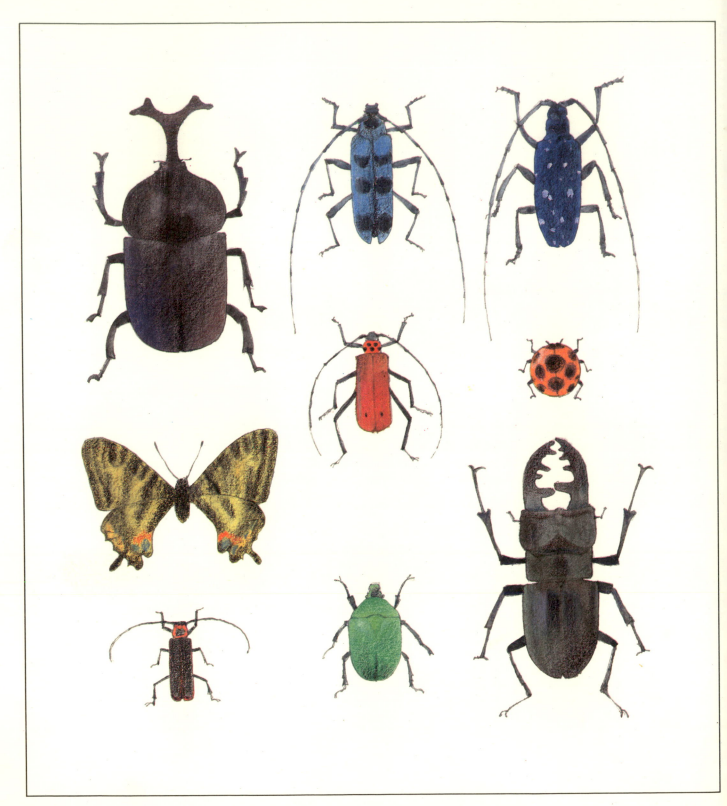

17

A baby frog is called a tadpole.
Can you find the frog and the tadpole?
Can you see the baby chicken?
Where is its mother?

Can you tell which one is different . . . ?

· 2 ·

Putting Together
And Taking Apart

A cat and a mouse are stuck together by their backs.
The cat can't pull away from the mouse, and the
mouse can't get away from the cat. Both are about to
go crazy. How in the world did this happen?

Our little friends, Kriss and Kross, invented a magic glue that can stick anything together. They stuck the cat and the mouse together with it.

Since olden times, people
have been sticking together
all sorts of things, and they
have come up with new
things—things that didn't
exist before.

Have you ever seen pictures
of mermaids and flying
horses? Such things are the
wonderful inventions of the
people of long ago.

Mermaids and flying horses are things that people put together only in their imaginations. But other people put real things together and made new things that were very useful. For instance, Kriss and Kross came up with the idea of getting lots of good-tasting fruits by sticking branches of sweet-tasting fruit trees to the trunks of bitter-tasting fruit trees. Look at the next page, and let's think what and what were put together to make what.

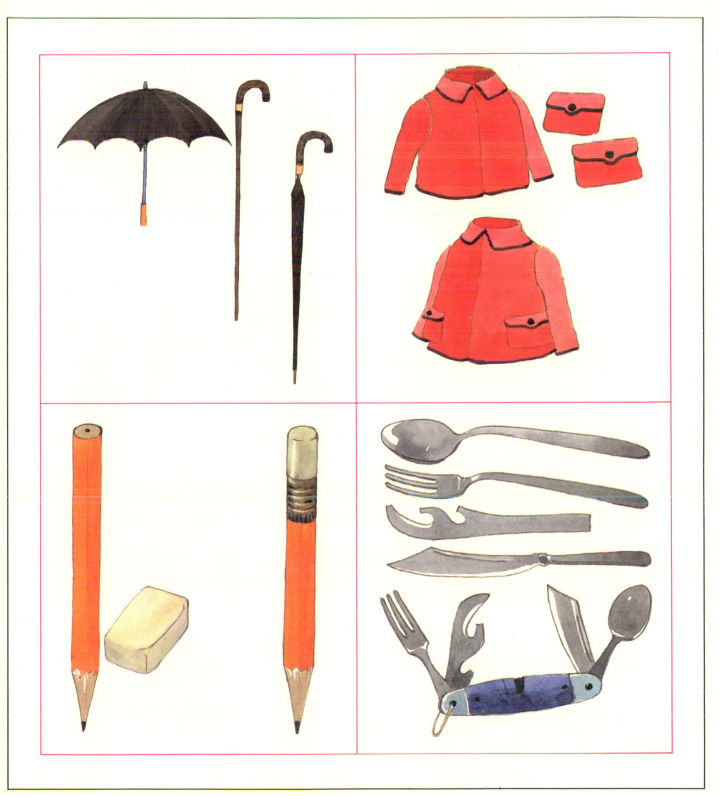

Here are some more put-together things. Let's think.
If you look carefully around the room you're in, you
will find all kinds of other things that were made by
putting together different things. Look what Kriss
and Kross have made!

Here, our little friends have put wheels on all kinds of things with their magic glue.

And here, they have put handles on a lot of things with their magic glue.

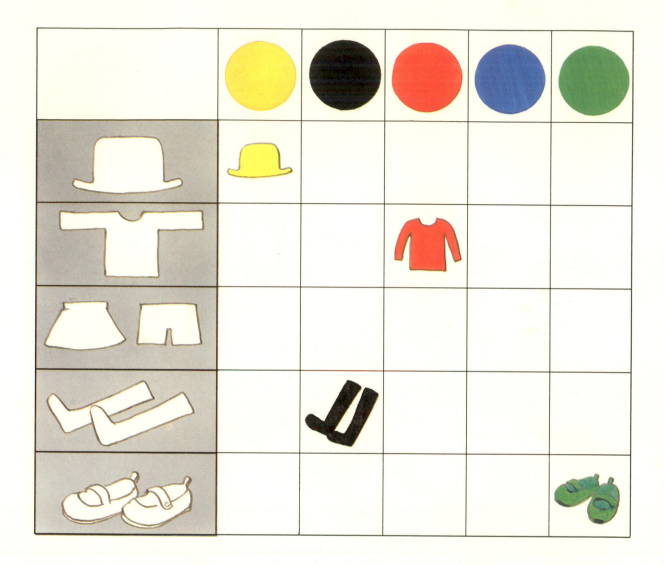

Now Kriss and Kross have colored some things to wear. There's a yellow hat in the square below the yellow circle. Which square does the red hat go in? Where do the blue socks go? Can you point to the right place?

Let's try to put each thing the children are wearing in
its right place in the chart on the opposite page.

	pocket	rearview mirror	chimney	string	bell	weight
(donkey)						
(elephant)						
(suitcase)					(suitcase with bell)	
(baby carriage)						
(doghouse)						
(cup and saucer)			(cup with chimney)			

Now our friends have put a bell on a suitcase. And they have put a chimney on a coffee cup. Let's try putting all kinds of things together. Let's see what kinds of things we can make. Point to a box and say what goes there. Then point to the other boxes one by one and say what goes in them.

	🥕	🐷	🐺	🌙	🐋	🍭
black						
hateful						
very tasty						
very big						
lost						
flat						

Now let's try putting together words and pictures. You will find some very strange things like a *flat moon* or a *black carrot*. Can you say what goes in each box?

Kriss and Kross drew lines on
a square piece of paper like this and cut it.

When they did that, that one piece of
paper became five pieces. The wind
scattered the pieces. They gathered them
up and put them together and made a
dog. They also made a factory, a fox
and a fish. How did they put the pieces
together? Why don't you try it, too?

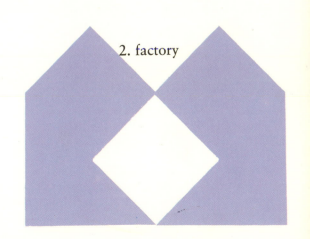

2. factory

1. dog

3. fox

4. fish

Here are some other ways to put the five pieces together.

5. fish

6. house

9. ladder

7. arrow

8. cat

10. clock

11. ship

13. crown

12. mask

14. flower

15.

16.

In this game, we don't just put things together. We also have to take them apart. Kriss and Kross invented something that separates things that are stuck together, and the cat and the mouse were finally able to pull apart!

Can you take these apart and get
the five pieces we started with?

17.

18.

19.

The cat and the mouse are glad to be apart!

· 3 ·

Numbers in Order

Our little friends are drawing a picture of a King.
They are making a deck of cards to play with.
The children are making cards too.

Finished at last!
But some of the children's cards are wrong.
Do you know which ones they are?

There are some mistakes on this page too. Look at the cards one by one and see if you can find them.
Then try to think how you can make them right.

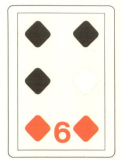

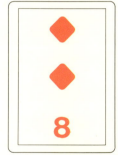

10   4   1   7   13

4   7   12   9   4

3   8   8   7   10

5   5   10   11   5

Look at the card which is fourth from the left on the line above. That's the Joker. How about the card fourth from the left on the line below—what card is that? Can you find the three of spades? Where is it?

Now then, look at the card which is fourth from the right on the line above. What is it? Look at the card which is third from the right on the line below. That's the twelve of hearts. The twelve is a Queen.

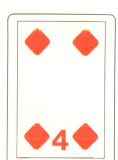

This is an apartment building.
Which apartment is the cat in?
Point to it with your finger.
The cat is in the apartment that is second from the right on the fifth floor. If you say it just like this, you don't need to point it out with your fingers. In the apartment that is third from the left on the third floor, there is a man yawning. Can you find him? What is in the first apartment on the right on the fourth floor?

Here are three buildings. In building number 3, the third apartment from the right on the second floor is the Joker's apartment. Can you find it? In building number 3, the fourth apartment from the left on the sixth floor is the apartment of the thirteen, or King, of spades. Did you find it? Push down lightly on it with your finger and while you are doing that, gently turn the page. You will see what is inside that apartment.

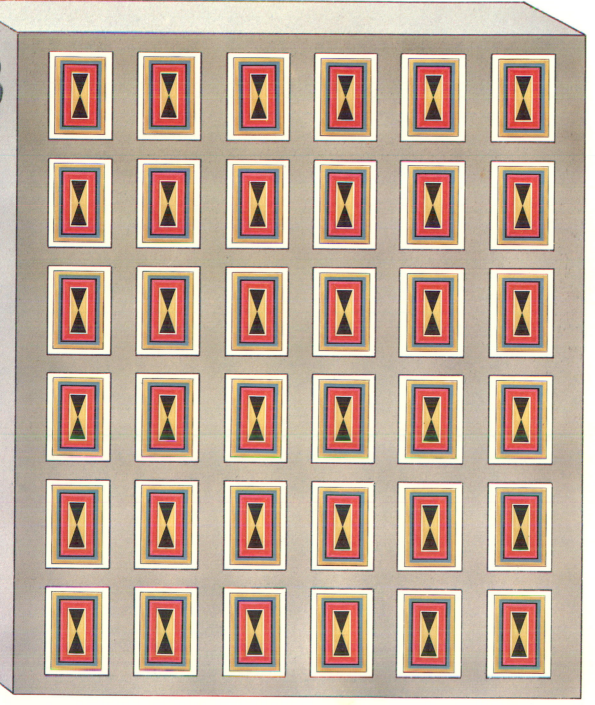

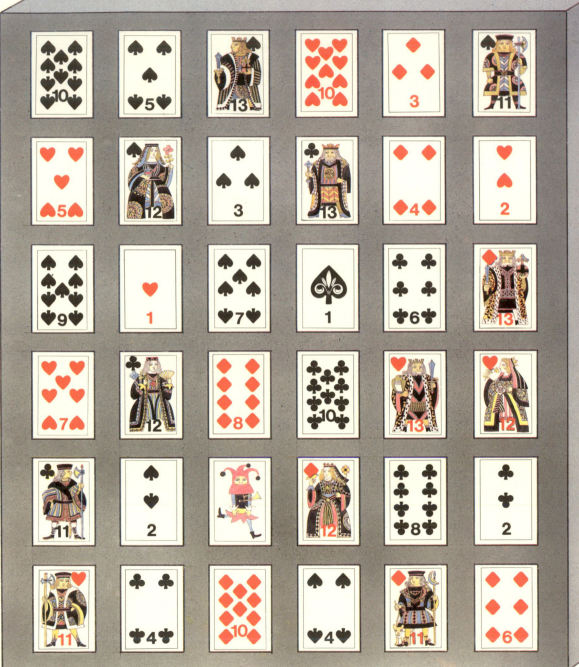

Here are four theater tickets. The location of the seat in the theater is written on each ticket. Where is each seat in the theater on the next page?

March 3rd

Row 4   Evening, 8 P.M.

♣ Section; Seat 3 from left.

March 3rd

Row 5   Evening, 8 P.M.

♥ Section; Seat 5 from left.

March 3rd

Row 7   Evening, 8 P.M.

♠ Section; Seat 4 from left.

March 3rd

Row 9   Evening, 8 P.M.

♦ Section; Seat 7 from right.

Have you found the seats?

Pick a place and point to it with your finger. Can you say where it is in words?

What kind of symbols do you need? What row—5th or 6th—from the front?

How many seats do you need— second, third, or fourth—from the left?

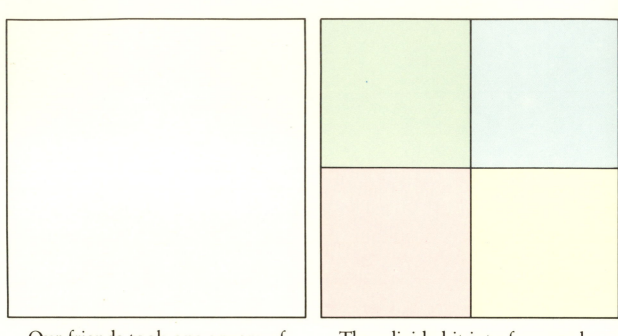

Our friends took one square of
paper.

They divided it into four, and
painted each section a different
color.

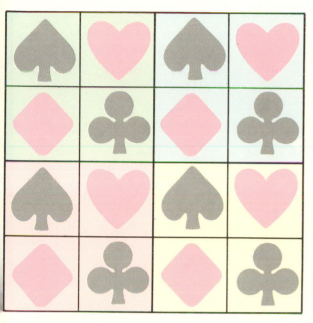

Then they took each colored square, divided it into four again and added the ♠ ♣ ♥ ♦ symbols.

Finally, they divided each of these squares into four again and numbered them from 1 to 4.

Now then—
Where is the blue diamond 3?
Where is the yellow club 2?
Where is the green heart 4?
And how about the pink spade 1?
Our houses are given addresses in just the same way.

See if you can give the
addresses of these houses,
using the same names as you
did on the previous page.

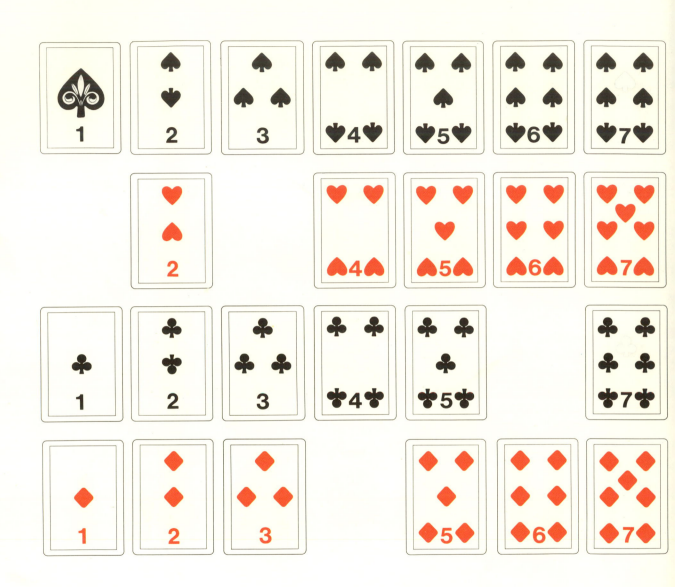

This is a card game called Sevens in a Row.
Look at the empty spaces. What cards should go there?

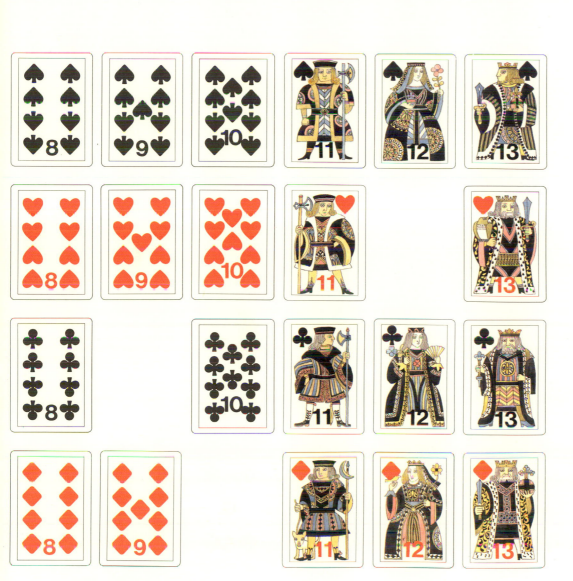

This card game is a lot of fun. Why don't you try it
and see for yourself? Directions are on page 99.

▪ 4 ▪

Who's the Tallest?

Kriss and Kross are trying to figure out which one is tallest. By comparing their heights, they can soon find out. But they can't compare their heights with their friends who live far away.

So Kriss and Kross make sticks that are as tall as each
of their friends.

Then, by collecting all the sticks, they can compare the heights of even their faraway friends. Let's think of the lines on page 75 as sticks. Can you see who's tallest? Who's shortest?

Now Kriss and Kross are playing a Japanese game. Each team is trying to get the most beanbags into the baskets. If we line up the beanbags in rows, like sticks, we can see which team has won, even without counting the beanbags.

We can think of this, too, as seeing
which stick is taller.

Here, Kriss and Kross and their friend are weighing themselves. See how the length of the spring changes. Let's think of the springs as sticks. The heavier the person is, the longer the stick will be.

Which child is heaviest?
Which one is lightest?

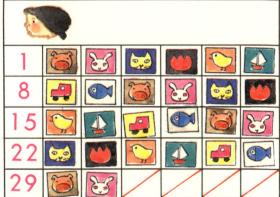

Every day when they go to kindergarten, these six children paste a sticker on the calendar. Kriss and Kross put each child's stickers in a row, like a stick. Then they can easily see which child went to school most often.

Here are many kinds of containers. Each one has some water in it. Let's find out which container has the most water in it.

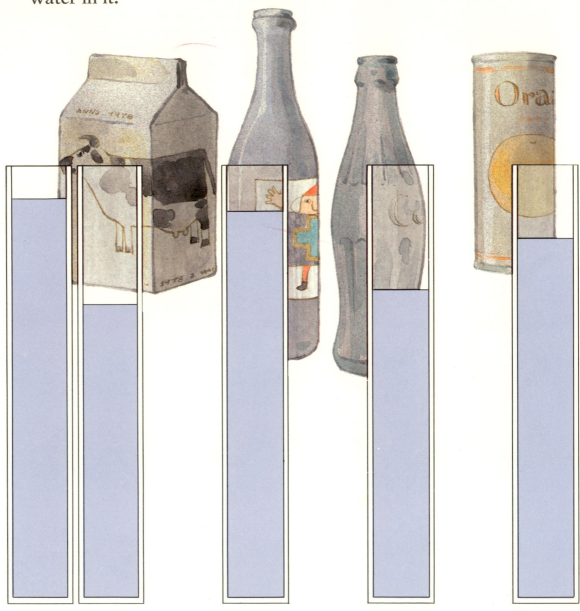

We can do this by putting the water from each container into long tubes that are all the same size.

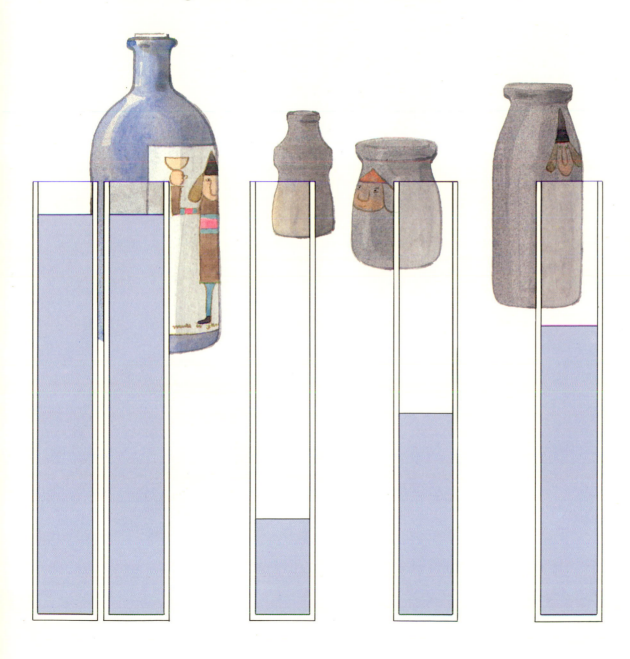

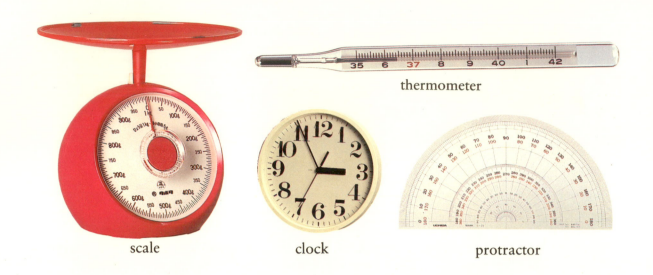

scale

thermometer

clock

protractor

Here are some tools. We can use them to find out such things as what time it is, how much something weighs or how long it is. But we can simply think of these tools as measuring sticks.

(Note: all tools shown are marked for metric measure)

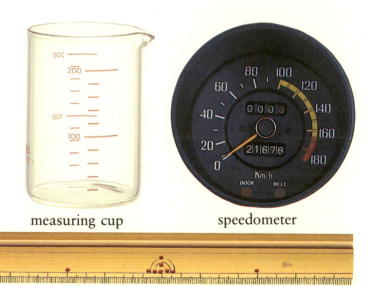

measuring cup

speedometer

ruler

Kriss and Kross found out that they couldn't measure
such things as "How scary is he?" or "How sad is he?"
with measuring sticks.

Which tube of water is sweetest? First, Kriss and Kross counted the sugar cubes in each tube. They think that if there is the same amount of water in each tube, then the tube with the most sugar cubes in it is the sweetest.

But what if the amount of water in each container is different?

Here are the same containers that appeared on pages 82 and 83. Each blue tube is filled to the top with the water from the container next to it. Kriss and Kross put some sugar cubes into each tube.

If we think of these tubes as measuring sticks, we can see which container has the most water. But how do you know which tube of water is the sweetest? Let's figure it out with Kriss and Kross.

Kriss and Kross put the tubes in order, from the one with the least amount of water to the one with the most water in it. Then they drew lines comparing the height of the sugar cubes in each tube. Kriss and Kross think that the tube with the highest sugar line is the sweetest one. Do you agree?

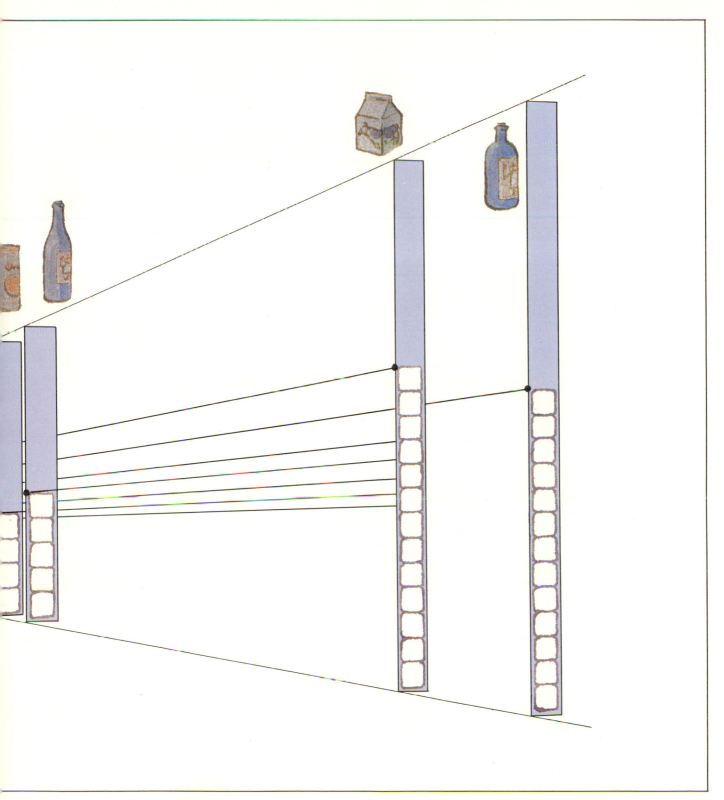

Here, Kriss and Kross drew lines to stand for the length of ten famous rivers and the height of ten famous mountains of the world.

Mt. Everest 8848 m (Nepal and Peoples' Rep. of China)

Manaslu 8156 m (Nepal)

Aconcagua 6959 m (Argentina)

Mt. McKinley 6194 m (United States of America)

Kilimanjaro 5895 m (Tanzania)

Mont Blanc 4807 m (France and Italy)

The Matterhorn 4478 m (Switzerland)

Mt. Fuji 3776 m (Japan)

Mt. Hodaka 3190 m (Japan)

The Nile 6690 km (Egypt)

The Amazon 6300 km (Brazil)

The Yangtze 6300 km (Peoples' Republic of China)

The Mississippi 3780 km (United States of America)

The Ob 3680 km (Union of Soviet Socialist Republics)

The Danube 2860 km (Rumania, USSR and Austria)

The Euphrates 2800 km (Iraq, Syria and Turkey)

The Rhine 1320 km (Netherlands and Germany)

The Seine 780 km (France)

The Tone 322 km (Japan)

If you draw lines or make sticks to measure with, you can find out which mountain is tallest or which river is longest. But the most important thing is that, like Kriss and Kross, you can find out fast with a graph!

· 1 ·

What Is Different?

*The Concept of One ·
Comparing and Classifying · Sets*

Is this really an arithmetic book? Many people have asked me this, and it is not an unreasonable question, for previously there have not been any arithmetic books in which children are asked to look for the similarities between ducks and beetles, or for the differences between elephants and birds.

Had I only wanted to teach arithmetic using the usual numbers and pictures, it would not have been necessary to write this book at all, for there are already plenty of books like that. But I wondered if I couldn't write a really new and interesting book, one that would teach not only the skills essential to the mastery of arithmetic but also a way of thinking that would have a bearing on *all* scholastic subjects. It would be a book that would share with readers the joys of creative discovery and at the same time occasionally throw them into a puzzling quandary. I realized that what this came down to was a book about mathematics.

While many people equate mathematics with arithmetic, its real meaning relates to much more than merely manipulating numbers. Above all, it represents

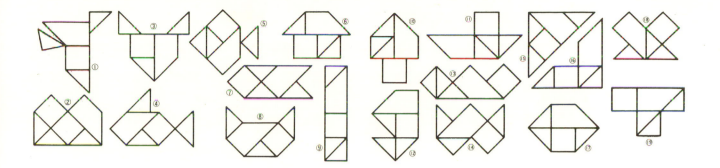

a way of thinking about things.

In the first section, my aim is to make the reader think about the real meaning of *one*. To achieve this goal, I have created several sets of objects. All the objects in a set, except one, share a particular characteristic. The reader must identify that characteristic and the object that does not share it. This is not always easy. Some of the sets are challenging, and I have included some for which there are two possible answers. This kind of comparing is basic to understanding many kinds of mathematical and philosophical problems.

When children cannot find an anwer, adults or older children should provide hints to help them in their creative struggle. It is through this process of struggle that children develop a mathematical way of thinking. When children finally reach a solution, they will feel the joy of discovery and will have taken the first big step in the development of their mathematical thinking.

Putting Together And Taking Apart

Combinations · Mixtures · Adding · Subtracting · Multiplicative Classification

Looking for imaginative ways of connecting one thing with another has been a method of creation and invention from the earliest days of the human race.

The ancient Greeks gave us the unicorn in their mythology. This imaginative and beautiful creation was an animal with the feet of a horse, the legs of a sheep, the tail of a lion, and a big horn in the middle of its forehead. In the Middle Ages alchemists used their melting pots to form their creations. Through various mixtures and combinations of ingredients they occasionally—and quite by accident—stumbled upon something. Today scientific advances are usually better planned than those of the al-

chemists, but there still remains a great deal of adding, or putting together, and taking apart in experimentation.

In mathematics, combinations or mixtures are produced by a process called *multiplicative classification*. The set of combinations is also referred to as the *Cartesian product*. For example, let us say that a child has two shirts (red and blue) and three pair of pants (blue, black, and tan). The following color combinations of shirts and pants are possible:

red shirt, blue pants
red shirt, black pants
red shirt, tan pants
blue shirt, blue pants
blue shirt, black pants
blue shirt, tan pants

These combinations form the Cartesian product. If one were only interested in how many combinations were possible, the answer could be found by multiplying 3 and 2 to yield the product of 6. This is the multiplication with which we

are more familiar.

While this more familiar multiplication is an operation on numbers, multiplicative classification is an operation on sets. This section will help children become familiar with multiplicative classification and the Cartesian product.

Some simple Cartesian products are displayed on page 29. For example, the Cartesian product of the set that consists of an umbrella and the set that consists of a cane, leads to an umbrella/cane. On pages 32 and 33, the items shown are the Cartesian product of the set that contains wheels and the set that contains familiar objects. On pages 34 to 43, the Cartesian product is produced from sets that have multiple elements.

As the examples proceed from the practical to the whimsical, readers are invited to join in the fun. Whether they recognize their creations in the world around them or only in their imagination, they will be developing important skills in classification.

▪3▪

Numbers in Order

Sequence ▪ Position ▪
Ordinal Numbers as Contrasted
with Cardinal or Set Numbers

Usually, we use the word *counting* without giving it a second thought. But if we really think about it, it is not that simple. In baseball, for example, the bases are called *first, second,* and *third* and not *one, two,* and *three* or on a calendar, the first three days of December are read as *December first, second,* and *third* and not as *December one, two,* and *three.*

Expressions such as *three days* and *the third day* are, of course, completely different. *Three days* indicates quantity. This 3 is called a *cardinal* or *set number. The third day* indicates an order or sequence. Therefore the 3 in December 3 is called an *ordinal number.*

To learn the concept of a set number, children need to have many experiences in *one-to-one correspondence.* Situations where children compare one thing with another must be provided.

Here is an example: Two children are playing with marbles and decide to see who has more. They match up their marbles one for one. When one child has none but the other still has some left, the answer is clear.

When children first compare things, they should be of the same type, such as marbles and other marbles, or people and other people. After mastering this basic form of one-to-one correspondence, children can compare completely different things, such as people and chairs, chairs and desks, or even people and stars. In this manner the abstract concept of "number" is being developed.

When children play the game of Put the Balls in the Basket, it would seem sufficient simply to shout "Yo, Yo, Yo!" instead of "One, two, three!" if the object is simply to see who has put more balls in the basket. However, if the point

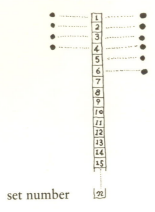

natural number

set number

is to see *how many more* balls have been put in the basket, children will have to count. In this counting, the child must make a one-to-one correspondence between the balls and the natural numbers (1, 2, 3, and so on). These numbers are set numbers, so if *five* is the number counted, it refers to a quantity of five balls. Be aware that although young children may be able to count to very high numbers, this may be an exercise in memory and perseverance only and may have very little to do with mathematical thinking.

As our image of mathematics is usually quantity oriented we are less likely to think of the ordinals. But when we speak of an order, a hierarchy, or of a progression, we are dealing with situations that involve ordinals. There are many instances where numbers show sequence and not quantity. Dates, page numbers, room numbers, and zip codes are just a few. These sequential numbers are very convenient. In fact, they are so

convenient that one could worry that numbers will some day be assigned to humans as well.

In the initial part of this section (pages 48–51), children are asked to find the errors on some of the playing cards. The errors include the incorrect number of symbols on a card. Children will be dealing with quantity and, therefore, with set numbers.

The rest of the section (pages 52–67) is mainly about ordinals, those numbers that indicate sequence. As you work with children in this section, try to avoid the temptation to ask questions dealing with set numbers. For example, asking "How many cards are there between the second and the eighth?" will only cause confusion.

As the children work through these pages, they will also be working with the concepts of left and right, above and below, and front and back. Therefore, be aware when the children look on page 58 for the answers to the card house

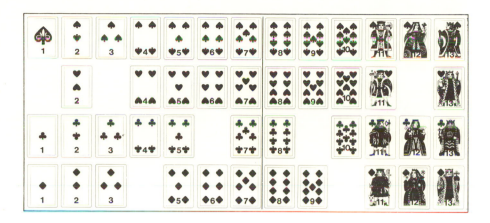

shown on the previous page that what was once on the right will now be on the left and what was once on the left will now be on the right. Children may find this disorienting at first, but from this state of disorientation they will eventually master the interrelation of left and right and of front and back.

When they have finished this section, I suggest that you and the children play the game of Sevens in a Row, which is based on the concept of sequence. You will need a deck of cards and at least four people. Shuffle the cards well and deal out all the cards. Players holding sevens should line them up vertically on the table. Then, taking turns, each player puts down one card to the left or right of a seven; these must be of the matching suit and in the correct sequence. (For more advanced play, allow diagonal placements as well as horizontal and vertical.) In other words, in the first round, sixes or eights will be played. Look carefully at the illustration to be sure you understand. When

a space is surrounded, as is the space for the six of clubs (shown above), the person holding that card may not put it down. The first player to use all of his or her cards is the winner. If all the cards cannot be played, the player having the fewest cards left is the winner.

∙ 4 ∙

Who's the Tallest?

Measurement ∙ Graphs ∙ Comparison ∙ Ratio ∙ Proportion ∙ Perspective

Measurements of length, mass, capacity, time, and temperature can all be expressed numerically, represented by a bar or a line, and then displayed on a graph. This may not seem important, but when you think about it, what this actually means is that we can take a concept that is not easy to grasp, such as time, and portray it by means of something we can see, such as a line. To take two apparently different things and make them

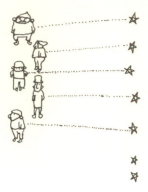

one and the same was a revolutionary concept when it was created, and is still a fairly abstract idea for children to learn. Yet all children today need to be able to handle this process with ease.

When a child compares the height of two friends, numerical values are not needed because the child can see who is taller. This is an example of a *direct comparison*. But if the two friends are in different cities, direct comparison is not possible. In order to compare them, numerical values must first be assigned to the height of each friend. This is called an *indirect comparison*. With indirect comparison, we are able to compare ourselves to people far away, to people of long ago, and even to ourselves when we were children. We also learn the significance of substituting numerical values for things. Using a graph, we can take these numerical values, transform them into lines and compare their lengths.

While graphs can be tremendously helpful, many graphs are of dubious value. All graphs deal with numerical values. But even though something has been given a numerical value, that does not necessarily mean it is measurable. Concepts such as happiness, or beauty, cannot be assigned *objective* numerical values. There are graphs that try to measure concepts such as these, but they should be looked upon with suspicion. I have seen, for example, a graph showing the rise and fall of the influence of the Tokugawa clan or the development of a sense of color in people. These so-called graphs are no more than types of pictures. They have nothing to do with mathematics, but at first glance, they appear to hold a kind of mathematically persuasive power, and that is something that bothers me.

Some *subjective* measures employ numbers purely for convenience, and it is important to understand that these have nothing to do with measured value. For example, gymnastics and diving are judged very closely at the Olympic

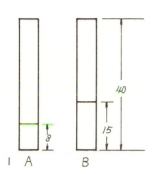

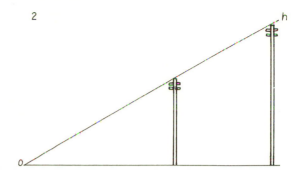

Games, and the performances are given point values. But these points are based on human subjectivity and are quite different from real measured values. In the same manner, school report cards are subjective measures.

Although we generally feel a kind of persuasive power when we look at a graph, we should look not only at the data but also at how the data was produced. In this way we can determine the real meaning of the numerical values. This should be kept in mind and impressed upon the children as you work together.

This section begins with simple linear representations of length, quantity, weight, and capacity (pages 70–83). Then it moves into graphic displays of the sophisticated concepts of ratio, proportion and perspective (pages 86–91).

Specifically, the section shows how to compare the sweetness of varying quantities of liquids. In order to do this, we must compare the individual ratios of water to sugar. It should be obvious that if two containers have the same amount of water, the container with more sugar will be the sweeter one. And if the amounts of sugar are the same, the container with less water will be the sweeter one.

But what if neither the amounts of sugar nor the amounts of water are the same? Things could get complicated.

Let us say that container A contains one gram of sugar and five grams of water while container B contains three grams of sugar and eight grams of water. To compare the sweetness of these two containers, we must create a ratio for each. The ratio of sugar to liquid for container A is 1/5 and for container B it is 3/8. By finding a common denominator of forty, we can use proportions to form equivalent ratios:

Container A   Container B
1/5 = 8/40   3/8 = 15/40

The new ratios of 8/40 and 15/40 al-

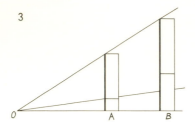

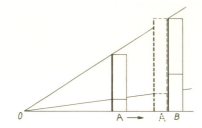

low us to make a comparison of two containers that have the same amount of water, namely forty grams. Since 15/40 (fifteen grams of sugar for forty grams of water) is greater than 8/40 (eight grams of sugar for forty grams of water), container B has a higher ratio of sugar to water and is therefore sweeter. *Figure 1* displays these new ratios in a graph. By making the bars of the graph the same height, we achieve the same effect as we did in forming the equivalent ratios.

We should be aware of a sense of proportion when we see things in the world and when we draw them. Seen from far away, a pole looks short, even though it may actually be quite tall. This same principle of perspective can be translated into a drawing. For example, if you take the pole in *Figure 2* and move it to the right along the diagonal line, it will get taller. But if you move it to the left, it will get shorter.

This technique can be applied to our problem of sweetness. Look at *Figure 3*.

Think of the two containers as being the same size but occupying different places along the diagonal line of perspective. A second diagonal line represents the amount of sugar in container A. Since this line falls below the sugar level of container B, container B is sweeter. (On pages 90 and 91 this method is expanded to include several containers.)

Explaining these concepts in words makes them seem very complicated, but if you see them represented in drawings of geometrical figures, they become easier to understand. It is not necessary for young children to understand the meaning of the words ratio, perspective or proportion. It is enough for children simply to experience an intuitive understanding of these concepts by using this book and creating their own geometrical drawings.

• • •

MITSUMASA ANNO is known the world over for his highly original and thought-provoking picture books, and in 1984 he was awarded the Hans Christian Andersen Prize, the highest honor attainable in the field of children's book illustration. A man of many talents and interests, Mr. Anno shares his enthusiasm for art, nature, history, literature, mathematics, travel and people with young readers through his uniquely imaginative books. He feels that the mathematical laws that underlie nature are as beautiful as other aspects of the wonderful world we live in, and that even very small children can understand and appreciate them if they are clearly and appealingly presented. In this book, which offers very young children a learning experience that is as enjoyable as a game, he demonstrates his belief that mathematics is more than merely manipulating numbers, it is a way of thinking, and that it has bearing on all scholastic subjects, indeed on all forms of creative thought. Born in 1926 in Tsuwano, in Western Japan, Mr. Anno is a graduate of the Yamaguchi Teacher Training College and worked for some time as a teacher before becoming an artist. He now lives in Tokyo, but he travels all over the world to do research for his many books.

Other Books by Mitsumasa Anno
published by Philomel Books

All In A Day

Anno's Britain

Anno's Counting House

Anno's Flea Market

Anno's Hat Tricks

Anno's Journey

Anno's Mysterious Multiplying Jar

Anno's U.S.A.

Socrates And The Three Little Pigs

Anno's Peekaboo

Upside Downers

Topsy Turvies

Anno's Faces

Anno's Math Games II

Anno's Math Games III

Anno's Sundial

Anno's Masks

Anno's Twice Told Tales

The publishers would like to thank Mr. Fred Balin,
of Balin and Lee Associates, and Ms. Jane Elliott for their help in
the translation and preparation of the text for this book.

Anno's Math Games by Mitsumasa Anno, copyright © 1982 by Kuso-kobo, first published in 1982 by Fukuinkan Shoten Publishers, Inc., Tokyo. All rights reserved. This book, or parts thereof, may not be reproduced in any form without permission from the publisher. Translation and special contents of this edition copyright © 1987 by Philomel Books, a division of The Putnam & Grosset Group, 200 Madison Avenue, New York, NY 10016. Printed in Japan. Published simultaneously in Canada. Philomel is a trademark of The Putnam Berkley Group, Inc. Registered in the U.S. Patent and Trademark Office.

Library of Congress Cataloging-in-Publication Data: Anno, Mitsumasa, date. Anno's math games. Translation of: Hajimete deau sugaku no ehon. Summary: picture puzzles, games, and simple activities introduce the mathematical concepts of multiplication, sequence and ordinal numbering, measurement, and direction. 1. Mathematical recreations—Juvenile literature. [1. Mathematical recreations. 2. Picture puzzles] I. Title. II. Title: Math games. QA95.A5613 1987 793.7'4 86-30513 ISBN 0-399-21151-9 10 9 8 7